Healthy Wrap Re

Packed with Nutrients

Portable Meal Ideas for Busy People

BY: TRISTAN SANDLER

License Notes

Let's get right into it because I wouldn't say I like fluff (you will see this in my recipes):

Why? I worked really hard to put this book together and, if you share it with others through those means, I will not get any recognition or compensation for my effort. Not only that, but it's impossible to know how my work will be used or for what purposes. Thus, please refrain from sharing my work with others. Oh, and be careful when you're in the kitchen! My team and I aren't liable for any damages or accidents that occur from the interpretations of our recipes. Just take it easy and stay safe in the kitchen!

ↄ◎◎◎◎◎◎◎◎◎◎◎◎◎◎◎◎◎◎◎◎◎ↄ

Table of Contents

Introduction

Wraps are an ideal meal for busy people. They will help you bring balance to your life with the proper mix of nutrients. Also, they are easy to grab in a minute. This recipe book provides 30 tasty wrap recipes to satisfy your busy life and taste buds. When you do not know what to eat and do not have much time to make a full course meal, all you need to do is scroll through the pages of the recipe book. You will instantly find something to satisfy your current cravings.

Preparing a tasty wrap can be done within 15 minutes. If you are feeling hungry and want to try a delicious dish packed with flavor and nutrients, let us get started!

1. Mediterranean Wrap

This wrap brings the authentic flavor to your table. The salad will add a touch of freshness, while the rotisserie chicken adds protein. You can get store bought rotisserie chicken and use it for meal prepping.

Time: 15 minutes

Servings: 1

Ingredients:

- 1 tortilla
- 1 cheese wedge
- ½ cup baby spinach
- 2 tablespoons basil pesto
- 3 tablespoons sun-dried tomatoes in oil
- ¼ cup rotisserie chicken, shredded
- 1-2 tablespoons feta cheese, crumbled

Instructions:

Lay the tortilla on a flat surface. Spread the cheese wedge over it.

Add the remaining ingredients to the center of the tortilla.

Fold the top and bottom edges gently, then wrap the tortilla tightly.

Cut in half diagonally and serve immediately.

2. Mozzarella Chicken Wrap

The combination of mozzarella cheese and basil pesto brings Italian flavor to your meal. This simple but delicious wrap will keep you full with the right choice of nutrients.

Time: 15 minutes

Servings: 2

Ingredients:

- ½ cup mozzarella cheese, grated
- 1 cup rotisserie chicken, shredded
- 1 avocado, pitted and sliced
- ½ cup canned artichoke hearts, chopped
- 1/3 cup basil pesto
- 2 teaspoons Italian seasoning
- 2 large tortillas
- Oil for cooking

Instructions:

Lay one tortilla on a flat surface.

Add some of the remaining ingredients to the center of the tortilla.

Fold the top and bottom edges gently, then wrap the tortilla tightly.

Repeat the process with the rest of the ingredients.

Brush with oil and cook on a heated grill for 5 minutes per side.

Cut in half diagonally and serve immediately.

3. Chicken Avocado Wrap

The chicken adds protein, while the avocado adds healthy fat. The vegetables will lift the flavor, while the sour cream adds a creaminess. This simple wrap features the balanced flavors and textures, creating the ultimate meal that will cheer you up during a hard work day.

Time: 15 minutes

Servings: 6

Ingredients:

- 6 large tortillas
- 2 cooked chicken breasts, sliced
- 1 large tomato, diced
- 1 cup sour cream
- 3 cups yellow sharp cheddar cheese, grated
- 3 cups lettuce, chopped
- 1 avocado, diced

Instructions:

Lay one tortilla on a flat surface.

Add some of the remaining ingredients to the center of the tortilla.

Fold the top and bottom edges gently, then wrap the tortilla tightly.

Repeat the process with the rest of the ingredients.

Heat a pan without oil. Then, grill the wraps for a couple of minutes.

Cut in half diagonally and serve immediately.

4. Buffalo Chicken Wrap

This wrap is an excellent idea for dinner when you are feeling lazy. It is way more manageable when you prepare the chicken ahead. Dress it with the buffalo sauce for an aromatic wrap.

Time: 25 minutes

Servings: 6

Ingredients:

- 6 large tortillas
- 2 cups cooked chicken
- 1 cup lettuce, shredded
- ½ cup buffalo sauce
- ½ cup ranch dressing

Instructions:

Combine the cooked chicken with the buffalo sauce and ranch dressing. Mix well to coat.

Lay one tortilla on a flat surface.

Add some of the chicken and remaining ingredient to the center of the tortilla.

Fold the top and bottom edges gently, then wrap the tortilla tightly.

Repeat the process with the rest of the ingredients.

Cut in half diagonally and serve immediately.

5. Avocado Turkey Wrap

The combination of deli turkey, provolone cheese and hummus creates an absolute gourmet pleasure for your taste buds. This recipe can use whole wheat or white flour tortilla.

Time: 15 minutes

Servings: 1

Ingredients:

- 1 whole wheat tortilla
- 2 ounces deli turkey breast, thinly sliced
- 2 tablespoons hummus
- ¼ cucumber, thinly lengthwise sliced
- 1 provolone cheese slice
- 1/3 avocado, thinly sliced
- 1 medium tomato, thinly sliced

Instructions:

Lay the whole wheat tortilla on a flat surface. Spread the hummus over it.

Add the remaining ingredients to the center of the tortilla.

Fold the top and bottom edges gently, then wrap the tortilla tightly.

Cut in half diagonally and serve immediately.

6. Hummus and Goat Cheese Wrap

Goat cheese has a pretty rich flavor so that it will complement grilled veggies. The result is a light meal that will keep you full.

Time: 1 hour 15 minutes

Servings: 4

Ingredients:

- 1 small zucchini, sliced
- 1 medium bell pepper, sliced
- 1 cup mushrooms, sliced
- 1 small red onion, sliced
- ½ cup hummus
- ½ cup goat cheese
- 4 large whole wheat tortillas

For the Marinade:

- 2 tablespoons olive oil
- 1 garlic clove, minced
- 2 teaspoons balsamic vinegar
- Salt and pepper to taste
- 1 teaspoon dried rosemary

Instructions:

Combine the marinade ingredients in a bowl. Whisk well.

Toss the vegetables in the marinade and leave them for 1 hour to absorb the flavors.

Grill the vegetables in a grill pan for 10 minutes or until cooked to your preference.

Lay one whole wheat tortilla on a flat surface. Spread some of the hummus and goat cheese over it.

Add some of the vegetables to the center of the tortilla.

Fold the top and bottom edges gently, then wrap the tortilla tightly.

Repeat the process with the rest of the vegetables.

Cut in half diagonally and serve immediately.

7. Turkey Club Wrap

When you are too busy and do not have time for anything, this wrap is your time-saving solution. Layer the ingredients and enjoy your delicious wrap within only 15 minutes.

Time: 15 minutes

Servings: 1

Ingredients:

- 1 tortilla
- 1 teaspoon mayonnaise
- 1 teaspoon mustard
- 1 cheddar cheese slice
- 2 lettuce leaves
- 2 cooked bacon slices
- 3 turkey slices
- 2 avocado slices
- 3 tomato slices
- Salt and pepper to taste

Instructions:

Lay the tortilla on a flat surface. Spread the mayonnaise and mustard over it.

Add the remaining ingredients to the center of the tortilla. Season with salt and pepper to taste.

Fold the top and bottom edges gently, then wrap the tortilla tightly.

Cut in half diagonally and serve immediately.

8. Turkey Cranberry Wrap

Consuming wraps every day does not have to be boring. This recipe will show you how to introduce a variety of flavors to your everyday meals. The combination of cream cheese, turkey and cranberry sauce is an excellent mix.

Time: 15 minutes

Servings: 2

Ingredients:

- 2 tablespoons chive and onion cream cheese
- 3 tablespoons cranberry sauce
- ⅔ cup broccoli sprouts
- 1 cup baby spinach
- ½ small apple, thinly sliced
- 3 ounces cooked turkey breast
- 2 tortillas

Instructions:

Lay one tortilla on a flat surface. Spread some of the chive and onion cream cheese over it.

Then, top with some of the cranberry sauce.

Add some of the remaining ingredients to the tortilla.

Fold the top and bottom edges gently, then wrap the tortilla tightly.

Repeat the process with the rest of the ingredients.

Cut in half diagonally and serve immediately.

9. Southwestern Chicken Wrap

This wrap gathers Southwestern flavors, packing them in a wrap for your convenience. The creamy and crunchy filling is ideal for rotting food after a long day.

Time: 15 minutes

Servings: 4

Ingredients:

- 4 large tortillas
- ½ cup tomato, diced
- 1 1/3 cups lettuce, shredded
- ½ cup cheddar cheese, shredded
- 1 whole avocado, diced
- 1 cup Fritos, crushed
- 2 cups cooked chicken, shredded

For the Taco Sauce:

- ¾ cup sour cream
- 1 ½ tablespoons taco seasoning
- ¾ cup salsa

Instructions:

Whisk the taco sauce ingredients in a small bowl.

Lay one tortilla on a flat surface. Spread some of the taco sauce over it.

Add some of the remaining ingredients to the center of the tortilla.

Add some of the taco sauce over the ingredients.

Fold the top and bottom edges gently, then wrap the tortilla tightly.

Repeat the process with the rest of the ingredients.

Cut in half diagonally and serve immediately.

10. Peanut Chicken Wrap

This wrap gathers exotic Asian flavors. The secret is the aromatic peanut sauce, which adds flavor to it.

Time: 15 minutes

Servings: 6

Ingredients:

- 6 large tortillas
- 3 cups coleslaw mix
- 1/3 cup roasted peanuts
- 1 cup carrots, shredded
- 2 cooked chicken breasts, chopped or sliced
- ¼ cup fresh cilantro, chopped

For the Peanut Sauce:

- ¼ cup honey
- ¼ cup olive oil
- 3 tablespoons unseasoned rice vinegar
- ¼ cup peanut butter
- 1 teaspoon sesame oil
- 1 tablespoon soy sauce
- ¼ teaspoon salt
- ½ teaspoon pepper
- 1 tablespoon fresh ginger, grated
- ¼ teaspoon red pepper flakes, crushed
- 1 large garlic clove, minced

Instructions:

Combine the peanut sauce ingredients in a small bowl.

Add the coleslaw mix, fresh cilantro, carrots and roasted peanuts to a large bowl. Add the sauce and toss to combine.

Lay one tortilla on a flat surface.

Add some of the cooked chicken breasts and coleslaw to the center of the tortilla.

Fold the top and bottom edges gently, then wrap the tortilla tightly.

Repeat the process with the rest of the ingredients.

Cut in half diagonally and serve immediately.

11. Chicken Bacon Wrap

Cheddar cheese, bacon and green onions are the ideal combination of flavors. You can consume this wrap straightaway or heat it in a pan to melt the cheese.

Time: 15 minutes

Servings: 1

Ingredients:

- 1 tortilla
- 1 cup cooked chicken, sliced
- 1/3 cup cheddar cheese, shredded
- 1 cooked bacon slice
- 1 tablespoon green onions, chopped
- 2 tablespoons ranch dressing

Instructions:

Lay the tortilla on a flat surface. Spread the ranch dressing over it.

Add the remaining ingredients to the center of the tortilla.

Fold the top and bottom edges gently, then wrap the tortilla tightly.

Cut in half diagonally and serve immediately.

12. Chicken Caesar Wrap

This recipe is for you if you love a classic Caesar salad packed with creamy dressing. The Caesar dressing, parmesan cheese and chicken create the antithetic flavor combination wrapped in one tortilla.

Time: 15 minutes

Servings: 1

Ingredients:

- 1 cup romaine lettuce, chopped
- 2 tablespoons bottled Caesar dressing
- ½ cup cooked chicken, shredded
- 1 tomato, diced
- 1 cooked bacon slice, crumbled
- 4 large croutons, roughly chopped
- ½ tablespoon parmesan cheese, freshly grated
- Salt and pepper to taste
- 1 12-inch flour tortilla

Instructions:

Combine the romaine lettuce, cooked chicken, cooked bacon slice, Caesar dressing, tomato, parmesan cheese, salt and pepper in a bowl.

Place the flour tortilla in the microwave for 10 seconds to heat it.

Add the Caesar salad and croutons to the center of the tortilla.

Fold the top and bottom edges gently, then wrap the tortilla tightly.

Cut in half diagonally and serve immediately.

13. Pesto Chicken Wrap

This wrap is aromatic and flavorful with zucchini, parmesan cheese and pesto. You will enjoy the fantastic flavor switching with every bite you take. Enough for 2 savings, double the ingredients if you want to enjoy it with your family.

Time: 15 minutes

Servings: 2

Ingredients:

- 2 tablespoons parmesan cheese
- 2 tablespoons tomato paste
- 2 tablespoons pesto
- 1 cup cooked chicken, shredded
- 2 garlic cloves, sliced
- ½ grilled zucchini, sliced
- ⅓ cup mozzarella cheese
- ½ cup spinach
- 2 tablespoon olives, pitted and chopped
- 2 tablespoon basil, chopped
- 2 tortillas

Instructions:

Add the cooked chicken, parmesan cheese, pesto, tomato paste and garlic cloves to a bowl. Toss well.

Divide the mixture between the tortillas. Top with the grilled zucchini, spinach, olives, basil and mozzarella cheese.

Fold the top and bottom edges gently, then wrap the tortillas tightly.

Toast in a pan for 3 minutes per side to melt the cheeses.

Cut in half diagonally and serve immediately.

14. Chicken Broccoli Wrap

Chicken and broccoli are a classic combination. You have the perfect wrap filling when you add a couple more ingredients.

Time: 30 minutes

Servings: 6

Ingredients:

- 1 pound cooked chicken, sliced
- 2 cups steamed broccoli
- Salt and pepper to taste
- 1 cup mozzarella cheese, shredded
- ½ cup sour cream
- 6 tortillas

Instructions:

Spread the sour cream over each tortilla. Layer the cooked chicken, steamed broccoli and mozzarella cheese.

Fold the top and bottom edges gently, then wrap the tortillas tightly.

Add to a heated pan and cook for 4 minutes until the cheese melts.

Cut in half diagonally and serve immediately.

15. Hawaiian Wrap

The combination of BBQ sauce and chicken gathers exotic flavors, bringing it to your table without much effort. This wrap brings a new flavor to your diet, letting you enjoy tasty food daily.

Time: 15 minutes

Servings: 4

Ingredients:

- 1 tablespoon olive oil
- Salt and black pepper to taste
- 1 pound chicken breasts, cut into bite-size pieces
- ½ cup mozzarella cheese, shredded
- ½ cup BBQ sauce
- ¼ red onion, chopped
- 2/3 cup pineapple, chopped
- ¼ cup fresh cilantro, chopped
- 1 romaine lettuce, chopped
- 4 tortillas

Instructions:

Season the chicken breasts with salt and black pepper. Heat the olive oil in a pan and cook the chicken until golden brown.

Remove from the stovetop and add the BBQ sauce. Toss to cover the chicken with the sauce.

Lay one tortilla on a flat surface.

Add some of the BBQ chicken, red onion, pineapple, fresh cilantro, mozzarella cheese and romaine lettuce.

Fold the top and bottom edges gently, then wrap the tortilla tightly.

Repeat the process with the rest of the ingredients.

Cut in half diagonally and serve immediately.

16. Cheddar Chicken Wrap

The mix of cheddar cheese, chicken and sour cream is something you will crave. With being easy to prepare, the wrap will become your go-to meal when you do not have much time for cooking.

Time: 15 minutes

Servings: 6

Ingredients:

- 2 cooked chicken breasts, sliced
- 6 tortillas
- 1 tomato, diced
- 3 cups lettuce, chopped
- 3 cups yellow sharp cheddar cheese, grated
- 1 avocado, diced
- 1 cup sour cream

Instructions:

Lay one tortilla on a flat surface. Spread some of the sour cream over it.

Add some of the remaining ingredients to the center of the tortilla.

Fold the top and bottom edges gently, then wrap the tortilla tightly.

Repeat the process with the rest of the ingredients.

Preheat a pan without oil. Grill the wraps for a couple of minutes to melt the yellow sharp cheddar cheese.

Cut in half diagonally and serve immediately.

17. Hummus Wrap

This fantastic recipe reveals a balanced flavor combination for an everyday meal with hummus. If you prefer a vegan version, you can consume it just like this. Or you can add shredded chicken for extra protein.

Time: 15 minutes

Servings: 4

Ingredients:

- 4 large flour tortillas
- 1 cup hummus
- 1 avocado, sliced thinly
- ½ large cucumber, sliced
- 2 small tomatoes, sliced
- 1 yellow bell pepper, sliced thinly
- 1 cup mixed salad greens
- 1 small carrot, julienned

Instructions:

Warm one flour tortilla in the microwave for 10 seconds. Spread some of the hummus over it.

Add some of the remaining ingredients to the center of the tortilla.

Fold the top and bottom edges gently, then wrap the tortilla tightly.

Repeat the process with the rest of the ingredients.

Cut in half diagonally and serve immediately.

18. Peanut Sauce Wrap

This wrap is rich in flavor and texture. The deli turkey enhanced with the aromatic peanut sauce will create a tasty meal.

Time: 15 minutes

Servings: 6

Ingredients:

- 3 cups coleslaw mix
- 1/3 cup roasted peanuts
- 1 cup carrots, shredded
- ¼ cup fresh cilantro, chopped
- 2 cups deli turkey, chopped
- 6 large tortillas

For the Peanut Sauce:

- ¼ cup honey
- 3 tablespoons unseasoned rice vinegar
- ¼ cup peanut butter
- ¼ cup olive oil
- 1 teaspoon sesame oil
- 1 tablespoon soy sauce
- ¼ teaspoon salt
- ½ teaspoon pepper
- 1 tablespoon fresh ginger, grated
- ¼ teaspoon red pepper flakes, crushed
- 1 large garlic clove, minced

Instructions:

Combine the peanut sauce ingredients in a bowl. Whisk until smooth.

Add the coleslaw mix, fresh cilantro, carrots and roasted peanuts to a bowl. Pour the peanut sauce over them and toss.

Warm the tortillas in the microwave for 10 seconds.

Lay one tortilla on a flat surface. Spread some of the coleslaw over it.

Add some of the deli turkey to the center of the tortilla.

Fold the top and bottom edges gently, then wrap the tortilla tightly.

Repeat the process with the rest of the ingredients.

Cut in half diagonally and serve immediately.

19. Spinach and Feta Wrap

Spinach and feta cheese are a tasty combination for a breakfast wrap. Enhanced with the egg scramble, this wrap will keep you full until lunchtime. Top with hot sauce if desired and serve immediately.

Time: 15 minutes

Servings: 1

Ingredients:

- 1 tortilla
- 2 tablespoons hummus
- ¼ cup egg whites
- 1 egg
- 2 button mushrooms, sliced
- ⅛ cup onion, chopped
- 1 tablespoon feta cheese, crumbled
- 2 cups baby spinach
- Salt and pepper to taste
- 1 tablespoon sun-dried tomatoes, chopped
- Cooking spray

Instructions:

Grease a pan with cooking spray and cook the onion and button mushrooms for 5 minutes.

Add the baby spinach and cook for 3 more minutes.

Add the egg whites and egg and cook for 2 minutes. Add salt and pepper to taste.

Warm the tortilla in the microwave for 10 seconds. Spread the hummus over it.

Add the scrambled egg in the middle and top with the sun-dried tomatoes and feta cheese.

Fold the top and bottom edges gently, then wrap the tortilla tightly.

Cut in half diagonally and serve immediately.

20. Mozzarella Hummus Wrap

Sometimes, the simple flavors are the best ones. The combination of hummus and mozzarella cheese creates a satisfying meal for your taste buds.

Time: 15 minutes

Servings: 1

Ingredients:

- 1 tortilla
- 1 tablespoon hummus
- 3 mozzarella cheese slices
- 1 tablespoon olive oil
- 1 handful spinach
- 3 thin tomato slices
- Salt and pepper to taste

Instructions:

Heat the olive oil and cook the spinach. Season with salt and pepper to taste.

Spread the hummus over the tortilla.

Add the spinach, mozzarella cheese slices and tomato slices to the center of the tortilla.

Fold the top and bottom edges gently, then wrap the tortilla tightly.

Heat a pan without oil and grill the wrap for a couple of minutes to melt the cheese.

Cut in half diagonally and serve immediately.

21. Crispy Tofu Wrap

This is a vegan wrap recipe that anyone will fall in love with. It shares a secret trick to make the tofu crispy and crunchy.

Time: 15 minutes

Servings: 3

Ingredients:

- 1 tablespoon avocado oil
- 12 ounces extra firm tofu, drained and cubed
- ½ teaspoon garlic powder
- 1.5 tablespoons cornstarch
- ½ teaspoon salt
- ½ teaspoon black pepper
- 2 tablespoons olive oil

For the Wrap:

- 3 tortilla
- 6 tablespoons hummus
- 2 cups lettuce, chopped
- 1 avocado, pitted and sliced
- 1 tomato, sliced
- 1 small cucumber, sliced

Instructions:

Combine the extra firm tofu, avocado oil, garlic powder, cornstarch, salt and black pepper. Toss well.

Heat the olive oil and cook the tofu until golden.

Lay one tortilla on a flat surface. Spread some of the hummus over it.

Add some of the tofu and remaining ingredients.

Fold the top and bottom edges gently, then wrap the tortilla tightly.

Repeat the process with the rest of the ingredients.

Cut in half diagonally and serve immediately.

22. Chicken Greek Salad Wrap

With the added chicken as a source of protein, this wrap is a satisfying meal for lunch or dinner.

Time: 15 minutes

Servings: 1

Ingredients:

- 1 tortilla
- ½ cup cooked chicken, chopped
- ¼ cup cucumber, chopped
- ¼ cup tomato, chopped
- 1 tablespoon red onion, finely chopped
- 2 tablespoons feta cheese, crumbled
- ½ teaspoon red wine vinegar
- 1 teaspoon olive oil
- Salt and pepper to taste
- ¼ teaspoon dried oregano

Instructions:

Prepare the Greek salad by mixing the cucumber, tomato, red onion, red wine vinegar, olive oil, dried oregano, salt, pepper and feta cheese. Toss to combine.

Add the Greek salad to the center of the tortilla. Top with the cooked chicken.

Fold the top and bottom edges gently, then wrap the tortilla tightly.

Cut in half diagonally and serve immediately.

23. Spicy Tuna Wrap

The spicy tuna salad is easy to prepare. When layered in a tortilla, it becomes a complete meal packed with unique flavor.

Time: 15 minutes

Servings: 2

Ingredients:

- 1 4-ounce can tuna
- 1 teaspoon soy sauce
- 1 ½ tablespoons mayonnaise
- 2 teaspoons Sriracha sauce
- 2 tortillas
- 2/3 cup carrots, shredded
- ½ cucumber, thinly sliced
- ½ avocado, sliced

Instructions:

Combine the tuna, Sriracha sauce, mayonnaise and soy sauce.

Spread the tuna salad over the tortillas. Top with the remaining ingredients.

Fold the top and bottom edges gently, then wrap the tortillas tightly.

Cut in half diagonally and serve immediately.

24. Cheeseburger Wrap

If you crave a cheeseburger, this recipe will satisfy your wishes. It brings the same ingredients packed in a tortilla for reduced carbs.

Time: 25 minutes

Servings: 5

Ingredients:

- 1 ground beef
- 1 tablespoon olive oil
- 1 tablespoon Worcestershire sauce
- 2 tablespoons ketchup
- Salt and pepper to taste
- 1 teaspoon onion powder
- 5 tablespoons cheddar cheese, shredded
- 5 tortillas
- 1 tablespoon mustard
- 2 cups lettuce
- 10 tomato slices

Instructions:

Cook the ground beef in a heated pan with the olive oil. Break down with a wooden spoon and cook until brown.

Add the ketchup, Worcestershire sauce, salt, pepper and onion powder. Mix, then reduce the heat to low and cook for 5 minutes.

Divide the cheddar cheese between the tortillas. Then, add the mixture.

Divide the remaining ingredients between the tortillas.

Fold the top and bottom edges gently, then wrap the tortillas tightly.

Grill for a couple of minutes on a preheated pan.

Cut in half diagonally and serve immediately.

25. Chicken Caprese Wrap

This wrap presents authentic Italian flavor with extra protein to make it a full meal. Take it with you at work and enjoy the flavorful meal instead of spending your money on sandwiches.

Time: 15 minutes

Servings: 4

Ingredients:

- 2 tablespoons olive oil
- 2 tablespoons white wine vinegar
- ¼ teaspoon salt
- ¼ teaspoon pepper
- 4 cups romaine lettuce, chopped
- 1 ½ cups cooked chicken, shredded
- ¾ cup fresh mozzarella cheese, chopped
- 1 pint cherry tomatoes, quartered
- ½ cup fresh basil leaves, torn
- Cooking spray
- 4 tortillas

Instructions:

Combine the olive oil, salt, pepper and white wine vinegar. Whisk well.

Add the romaine lettuce, cooked chicken, fresh mozzarella cheese, fresh basil leaves and cherry tomatoes.

Coat a pan with cooking spray. Grill the tortillas for 1 minute per side.

Arrange the mixture in the center of each tortilla.

Fold the top and bottom edges gently, then wrap the tortillas tightly.

Cut in half diagonally and serve immediately.

26. Mexican Tortilla Wrap

The quinoa will keep you full for longer, while the black beans and corn add extra nutrients. The spices will bring authentic Mexican flavor, creating a tasty and portable meal. Serve with guacamole for an authentic feel.

Time: 25 minutes

Servings: 6

Ingredients:

- 2 cups cooked quinoa
- 15 ounces black beans
- 7 ounces corn
- 1 onion, chopped
- 1 red pepper, diced
- Salt and pepper to taste
- 3 tablespoons BBQ sauce
- 6 tortillas
- Oil for cooking

Instructions:

Cook the onion and red pepper in heated oil in a pan.

Divide the cooked quinoa between the tortillas. Add the mixture, corn and black beans.

Top with the BBQ sauce.

Fold the top and bottom edges gently, then wrap the tortillas tightly.

Cut in half diagonally and serve immediately.

27. Turkey Bacon Wrap

With turkey bacon and deli turkey, this recipe is tasty and low in fat. The 5-ingredient wrap is easy and simple to make, which is ideal for busy days when you do not have time to cook a meal.

Time: 15 minutes

Servings: 8

Ingredients:

- 6 tortillas
- 6 tablespoons ranch dressing
- 1 ½ pounds deli turkey, sliced
- 18 cooked turkey bacon strips
- 6 romaine lettuce leaves

Instructions:

Lay one tortilla on a flat surface. Spread some of the ranch dressing over it.

Add some of the remaining ingredients to the tortilla.

Fold the top and bottom edges gently, then wrap the tortilla tightly.

Repeat the process with the rest of the ingredients.

Cut in half diagonally and serve immediately.

28. Turkey Avocado Wrap

Smoked deli turkey wrapped in layers of cheddar cheese, Roma tomato and avocado is a delicious combination. Serve this wrap with air fryer fries for a tasty and guilt-free pleasure.

Time: 15 minutes

Servings: 4

Ingredients:

- 4 large tortillas
- 8 tablespoons ranch dressing
- 8 sharp cheddar cheese slices
- 8 ounces smoked deli turkey breast
- 2 roma tomatoes, sliced
- 4 large lettuce leaves
- 1 avocado, cut into thin pieces

Instructions:

Lay one tortilla on a flat surface. Spread some of the ranch dressing over it.

Add some of the remaining ingredients to the center of the tortilla.

Fold the top and bottom edges gently, then wrap the tortilla tightly.

Repeat the process with the rest of the ingredients.

Cut in half diagonally and serve immediately.

29. Salmon Cream Cheese Wrap

With smoked salmon, basil and arugula, this wrap recipe is a real delicacy. The ingredients are enough for one wrap, but you can add more for meal prepping for others.

Time: 15 minutes

Servings: 1

Ingredients:

- 1 tortilla
- 2 teaspoons cream cheese
- 2 ounces smoked salmon
- 1 ¼ ounces red onion
- ½ cup arugula
- ½ teaspoon fresh or dried basil
- ¼ teaspoon pepper

Instructions:

Warm the tortilla in the microwave for 10 seconds.

Mix the cream cheese with the basil and pepper.

Lay the tortilla on a flat surface. Spread the cream cheese over it.

Add the remaining ingredients to the center of the tortilla.

Fold the top and bottom edges gently, then wrap the tortilla tightly.

Cut in half diagonally and serve immediately.

30. Mediterranean Wrap

This delicious wrap is layered with tasty Mediterranean salad and spicy fried chickpeas. The secret is that the chickpeas are packed with flavor.

Time: 25 minutes

Servings: 4

Ingredients:

- 1 cup canned chickpeas, rinsed and drained
- ½ teaspoon dried mint
- 2 garlic cloves, minced
- 1 tablespoon lemon juice
- 1 ½ tablespoons tahini
- 2 tablespoons water
- 1 tablespoon olive oil
- 1 teaspoon crushed red pepper
- 4 tablespoons tomato
- 4 tablespoons cucumber
- 4 tablespoons avocado, chopped
- ½ cup spinach
- 4 tablespoons hummus
- 4 small tortillas

Instructions:

Heat the olive oil at medium heat. Fry the canned chickpeas with the crushed red pepper, dried mint and garlic clove.

Mix the tahini, garlic clove and lemon juice. Thin the sauce with the water or more to your preference.

Lay one tortilla on a flat surface. Spread some of the hummus over it.

Add some of the sauce and remaining ingredients to the center of the tortilla.

Fold the top and bottom edges gently, then wrap the tortilla tightly.

Repeat the process with the rest of the ingredients.

Cut in half diagonally and serve immediately.

Conclusion

With these healthy wrap recipes, you are one step closer to having the life you want. The balanced meals will keep you full during the day while being easy to move. You can explore the variety of flavors and never get tired of them. With the 30 wrap recipes, you can eat different dishes every day. Whether you prefer chicken or turkey, or a vegetarian option, you can always find the right match for your current cravings. The healthy wraps make meal prepping way easier for you.

Healthy Wrap Recipes Packed with Nutrients is not just a recipe book. It will motivate you to eat healthy food, with plenty of inspiration for the moments you do not know what to eat. Also, it will show you how to prepare meals with simple ingredients. You will get to save money by preparing your food at home.

If you liked the recipe book, do not mind checking the others in our collection. We are sure that you will find the right fit for your taste!

Author's Afterthoughts

thank you

Now's the moment of truth… What did you think about my cookbook? Did you like the recipes in it? While I certainly hope so, I would also like to know what you'd like to see more of! This might come as a surprise to you, but your ideas will surely inspire my upcoming cookbooks since the only reason I write is so that you can try out my dishes! Without you, I certainly wouldn't be here–writing and all.

Perhaps you'd like a cookbook to help you with weight loss or to help you stick to the Keto diet while eating delicious meals…Or maybe you'd just like to see a whole cookbook on brunch recipes or overnight breakfasts… You're the boss!

The only reason I can write cookbooks and try new recipes for a living is because of you, so now is my time to show some gratitude by creating cookbooks that will actually help you get through your weekly meals or special occasions! Just let us know what you'd like to see more of, and you can bet we'll get your ideas to the drawing board.

Thanks,

Tristan

About the Author

Tristan grew up watching his dad and grandma spend hours in the kitchen before a family gathering. They would prepare some of granny's secret family recipes together and then serve them once everyone arrived. Tristan only chopped carrots and onions for them, occasionally stirring the pots too, but he didn't realize how important his job was until he grew up and found himself needing a hand in the kitchen.

Especially when living on your own, doing all the chopping and cooking yourself can be very tiring. While he wished his cat could lend him a paw, hairballs weren't exactly part of his weekly night menu. For some time, Tristan lived off take-out food because it was convenient. After a long day of work, who wants to spend another hour preparing dinner and then washing the dishes? It wasn't until a buddy of his, who also happened to live on his own, introduced him into the world of meal preps and easy, simple dinners that Tristan's life changed.

He started cooking for himself. Nothing fancy, just quick but healthy meals that didn't make him dread coming home to make dinner. The cleanup was easy, too, since it was mostly one-pot meals. Eventually, he started to freeze his meals for the entire month, only reheating them as needed. His colleagues started to pick up on this, and they were soon asking Tristan to make their weekly lunch and dinners too!

Though he never envisioned himself as a full-time cook, Tristan now runs his own meal prep company in California, preparing over 1,000 meals per week for busy people who want healthy homemade meals. Occasionally, his dad goes to help out in the kitchen, now only letting him chop carrots and onions, occasionally stirring the pots too, and Tristan can't believe how lucky he is to have a helping hand like his.

)◎◎◎◎◎◎◎◎◎◎◎◎◎◎◎◎◎◎◎◎◎(

Printed in Great Britain
by Amazon

22651788R00044